COLOR YOUR RIGHTS

I'M WITH HER, YOU'RE WITH ME,

We're all in this together

30 PAGE COLORING BOOK

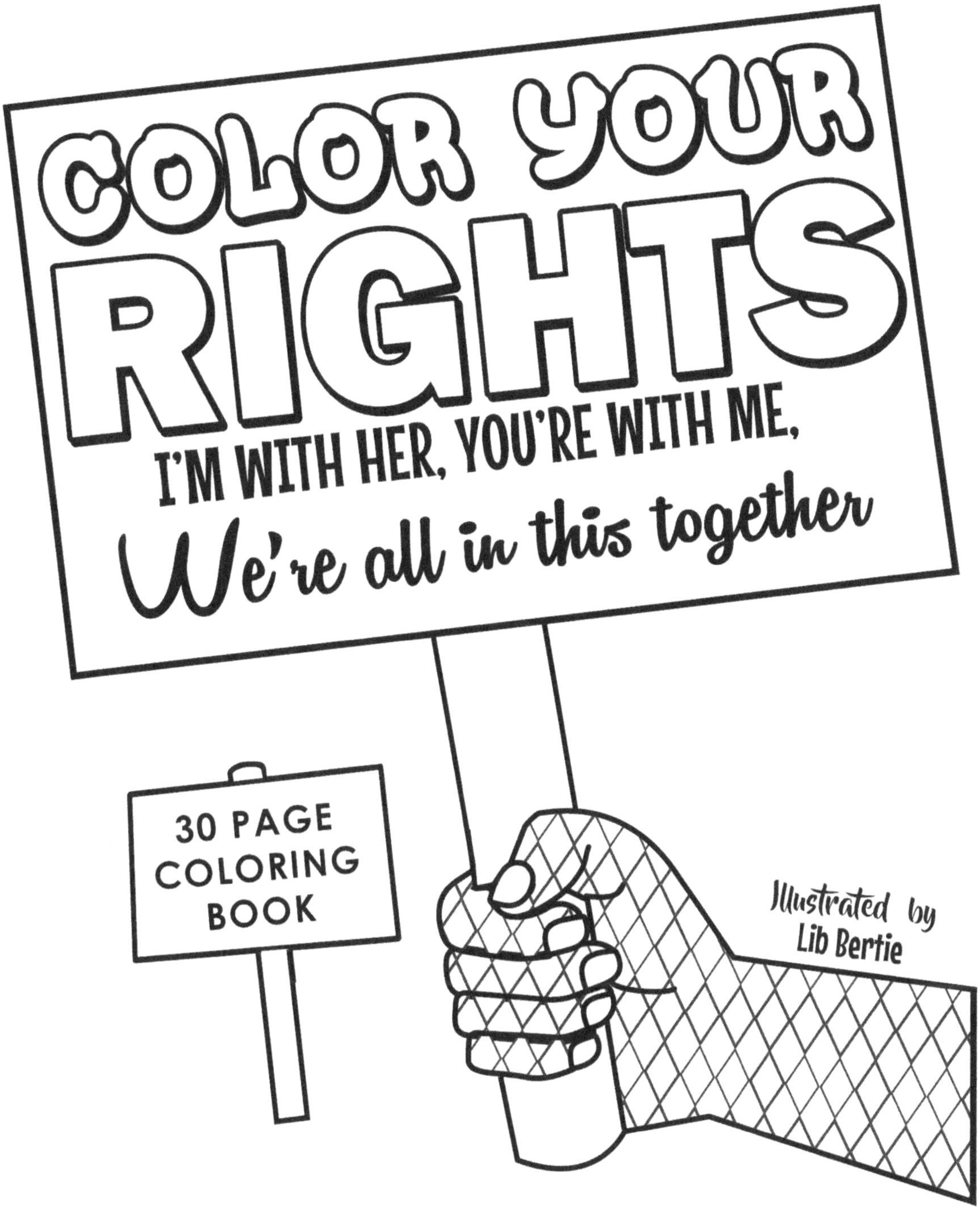

Illustrated by
Lib Bertie

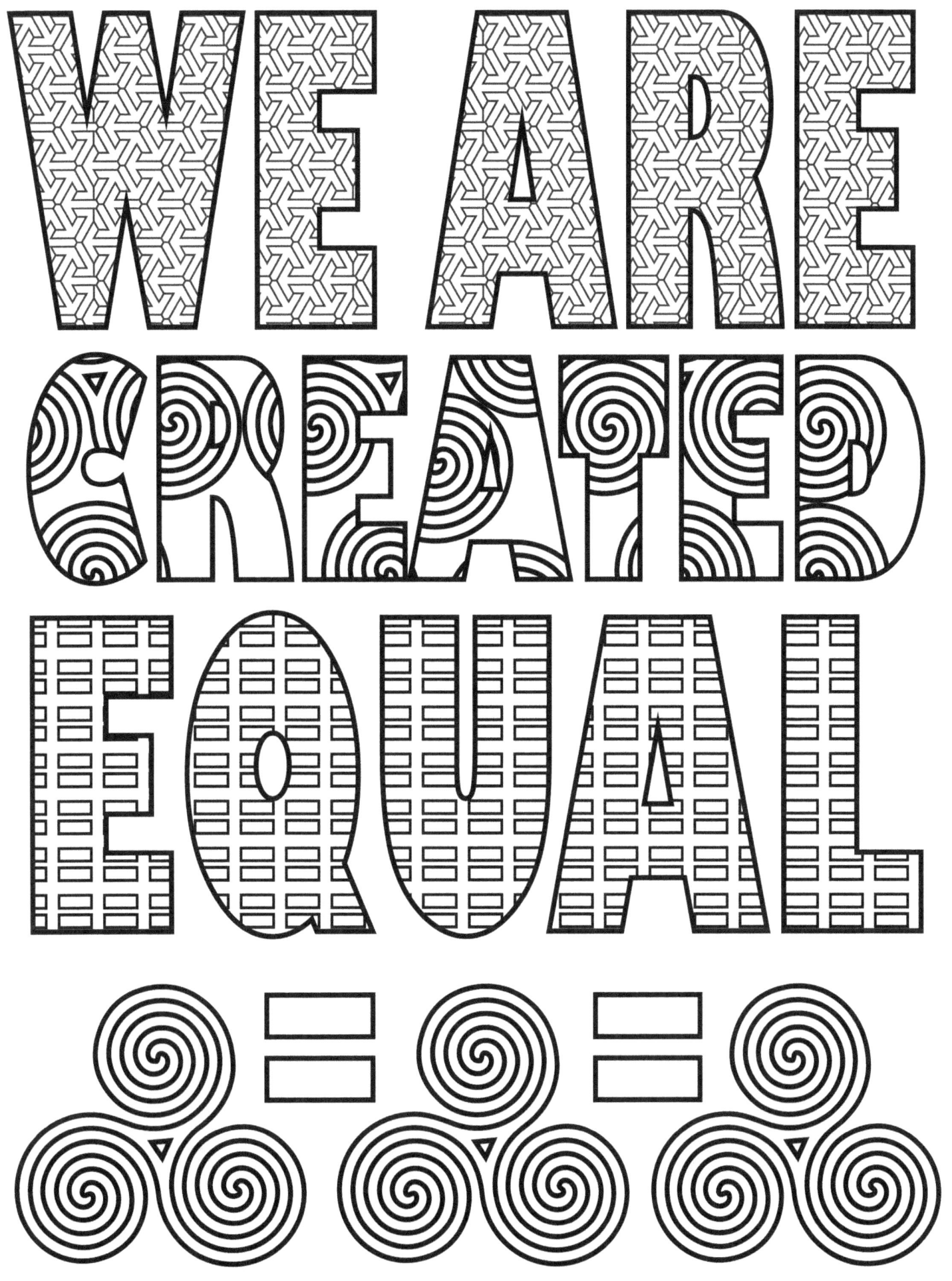

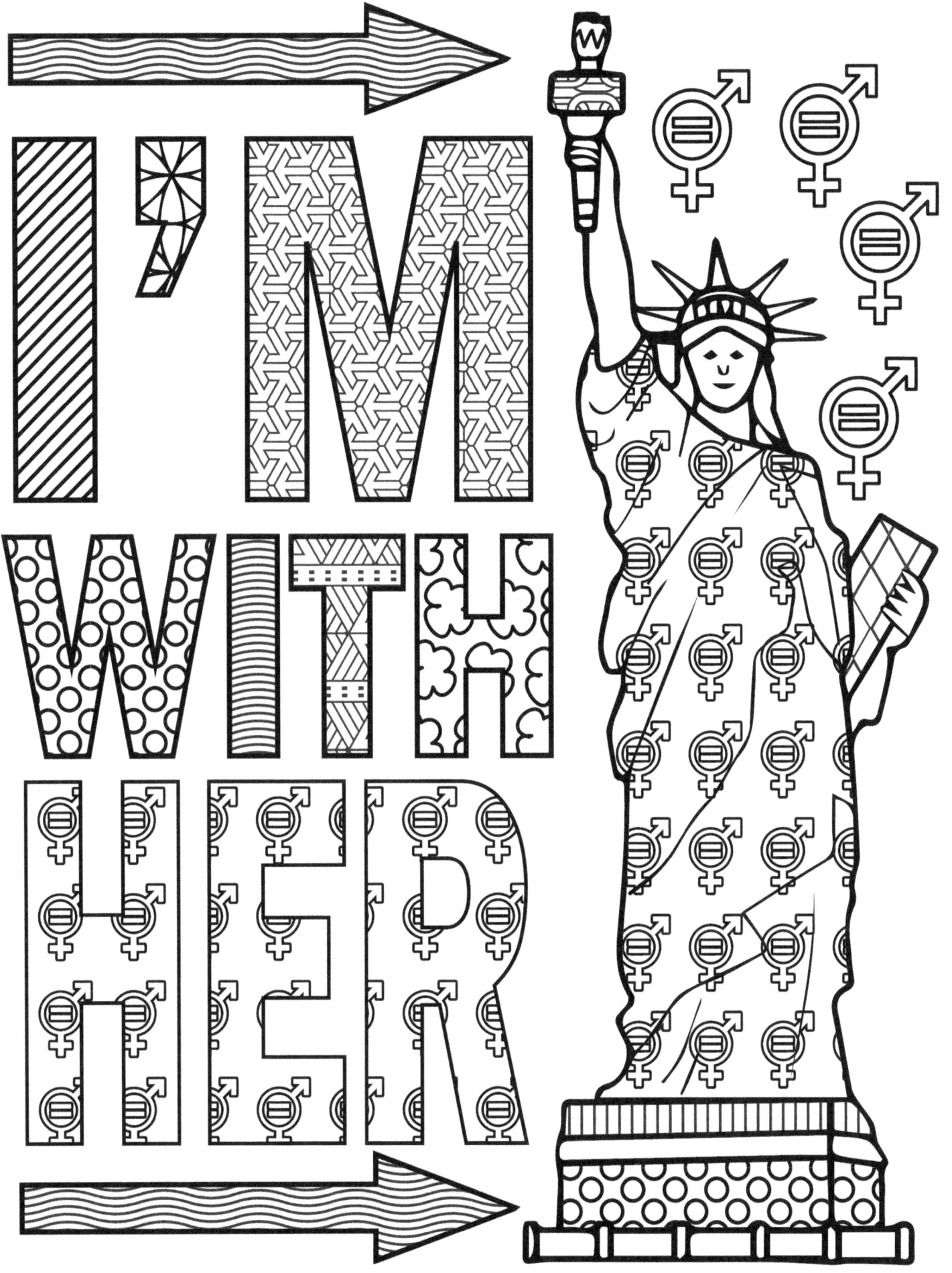

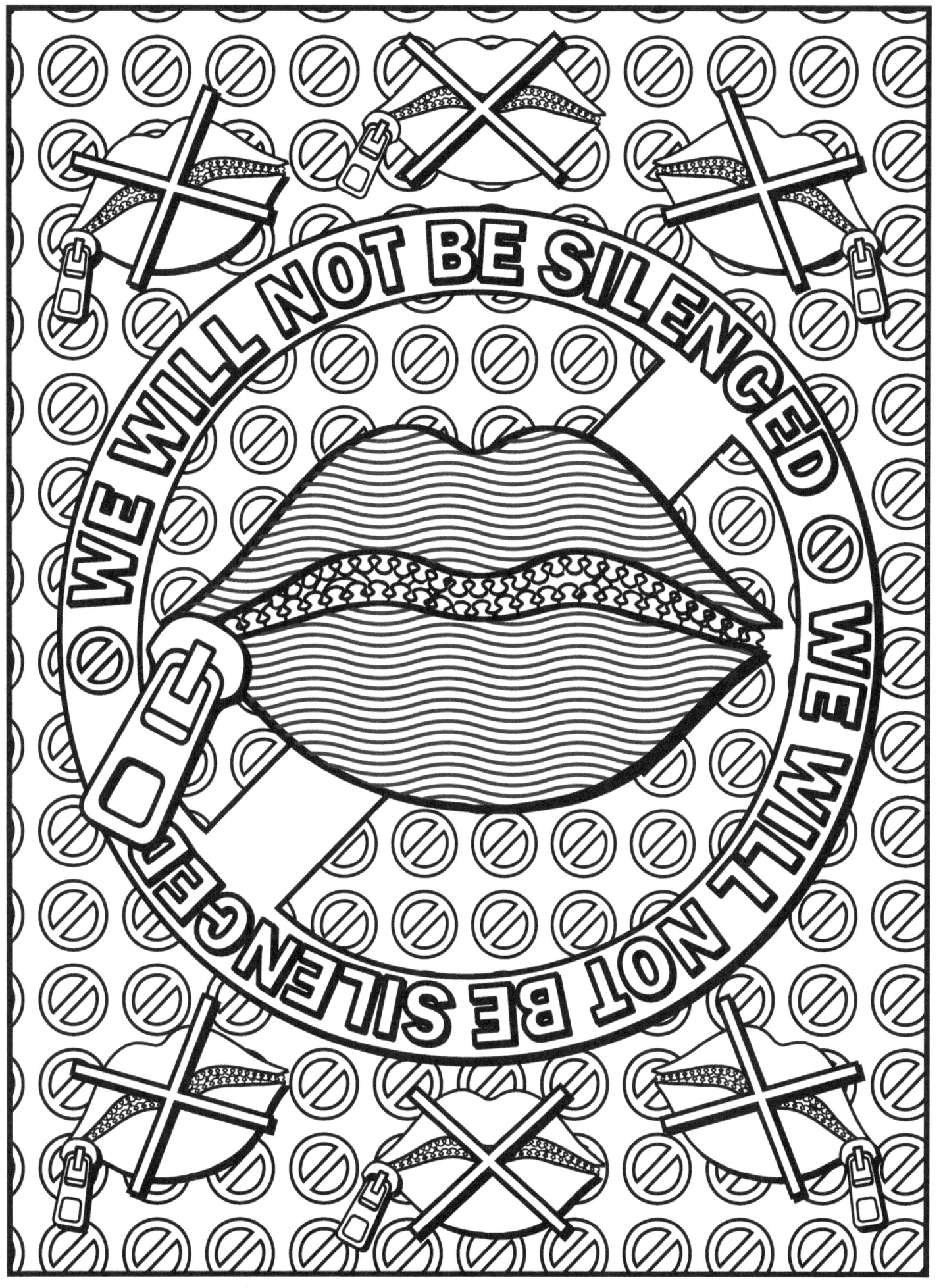

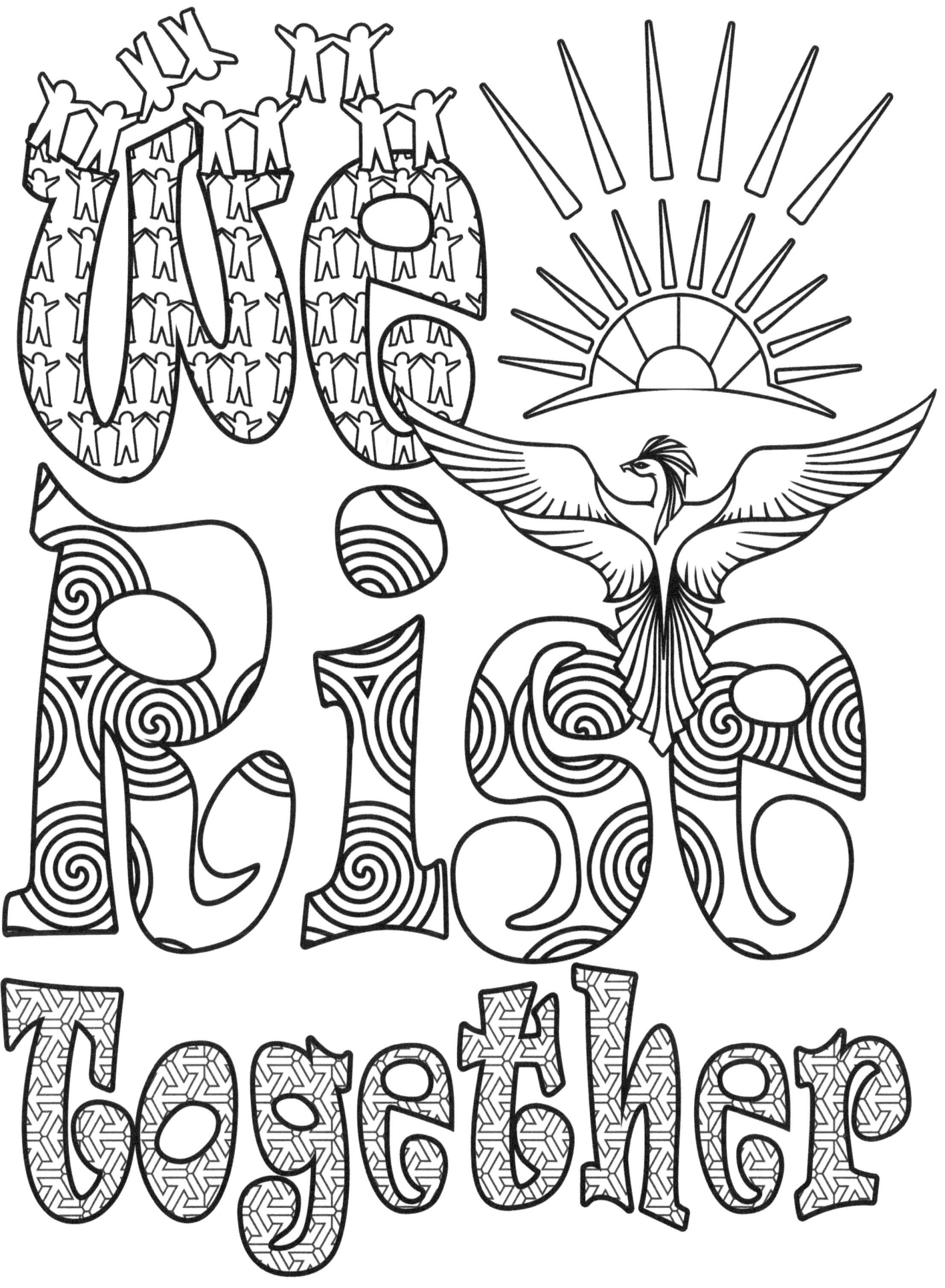

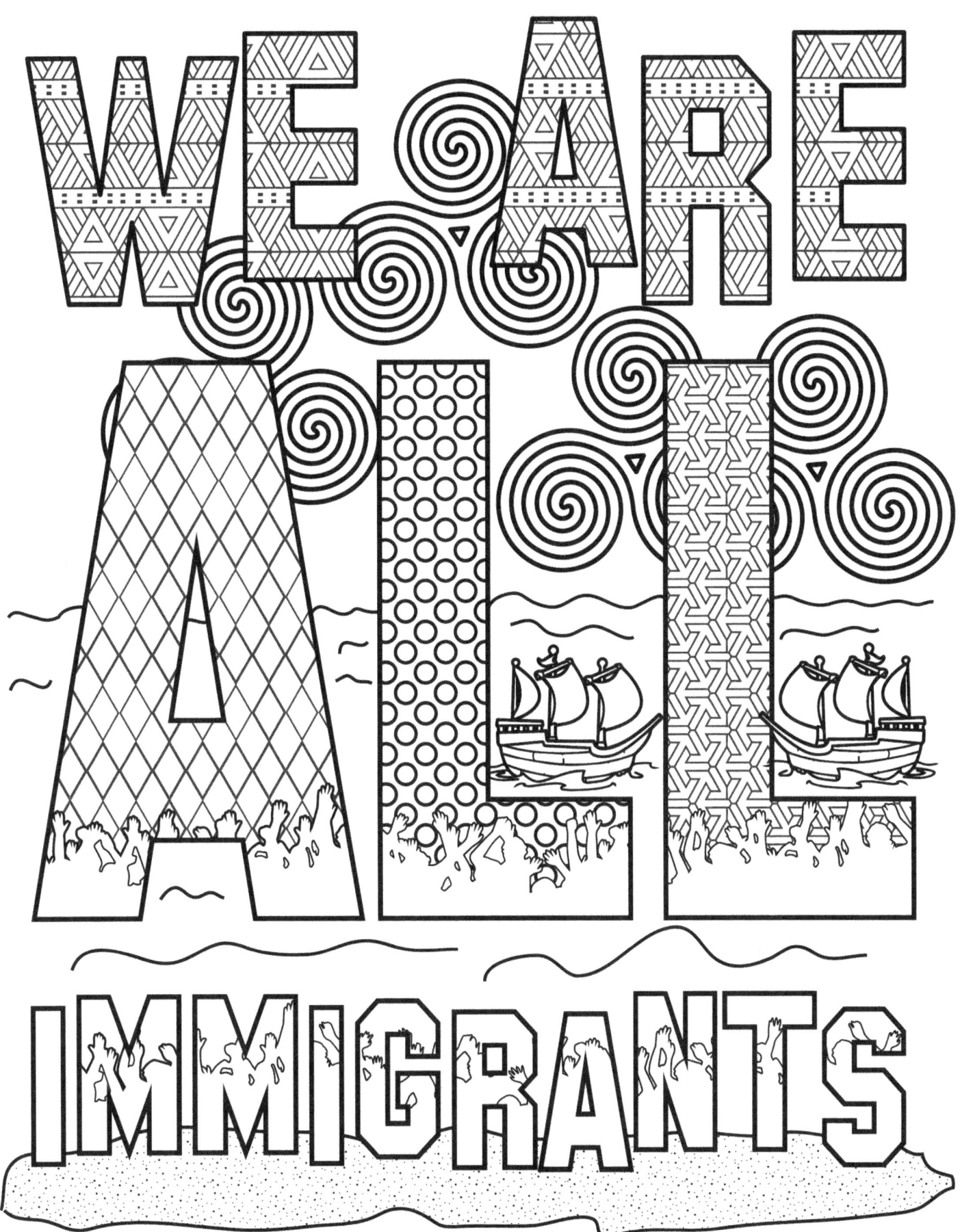

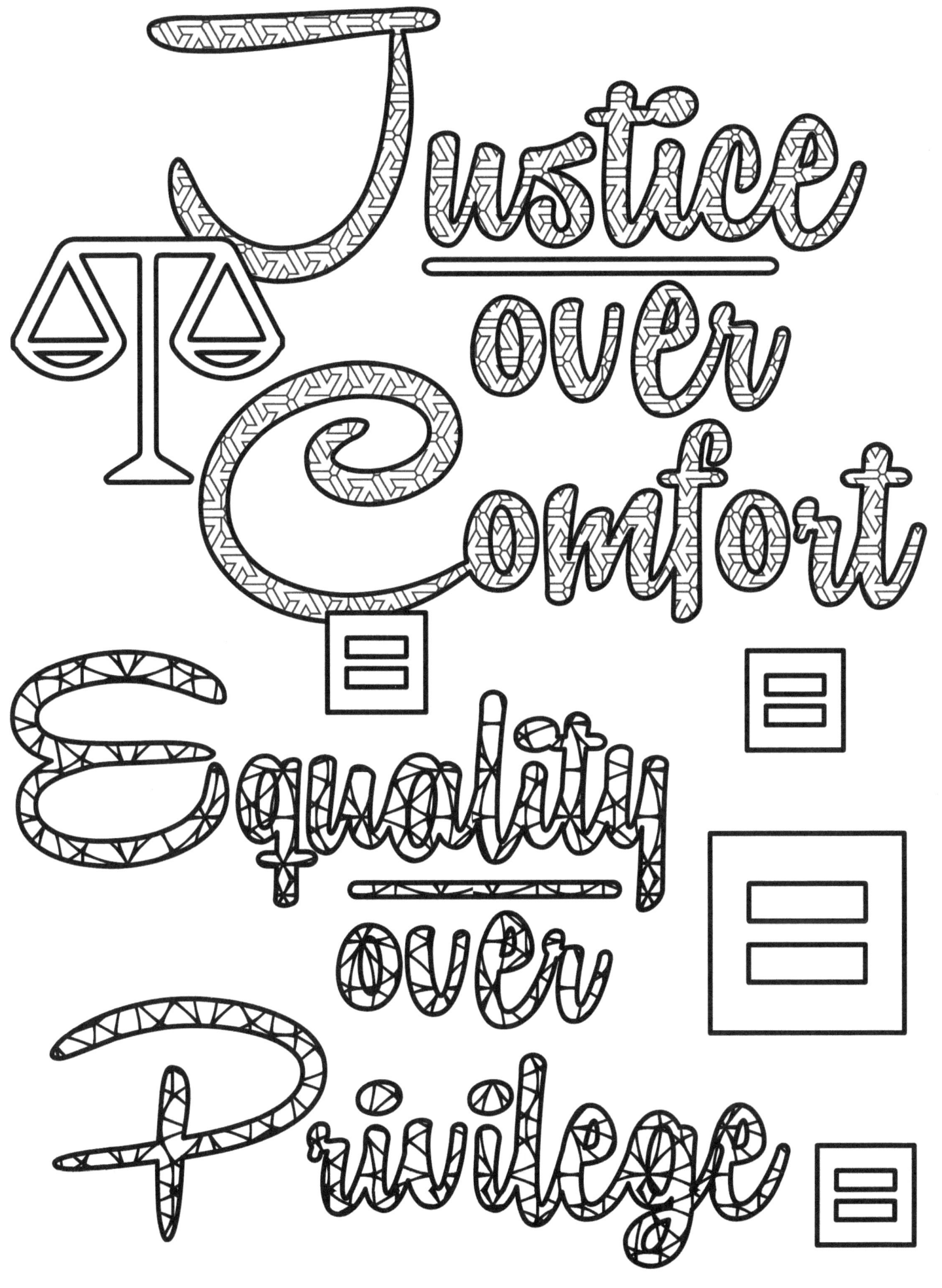

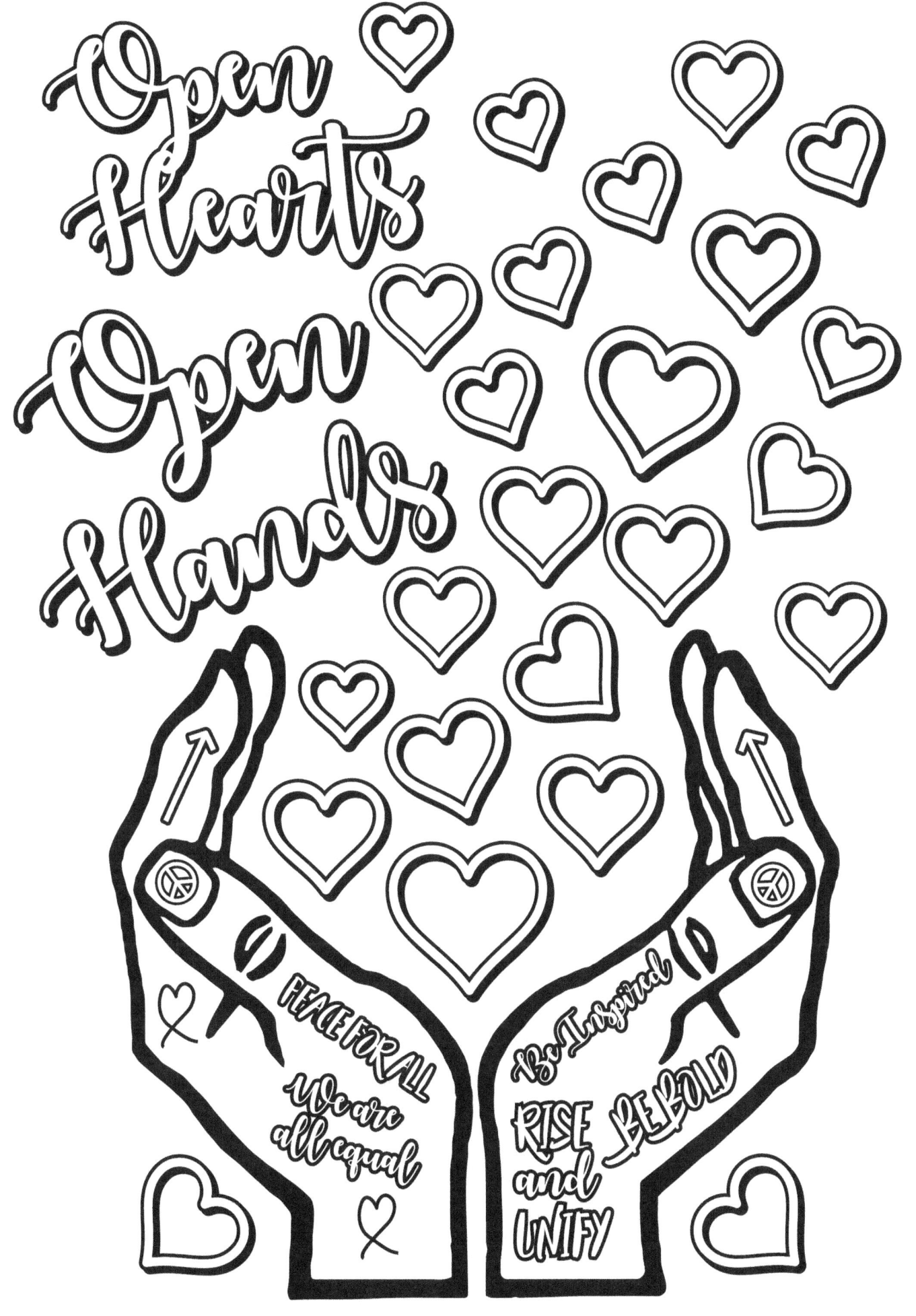

Express Yourself

SAY SOMETHING. DRAW IT. WRITE IT. OR TAKE A PICTURE AND TYPE IT.

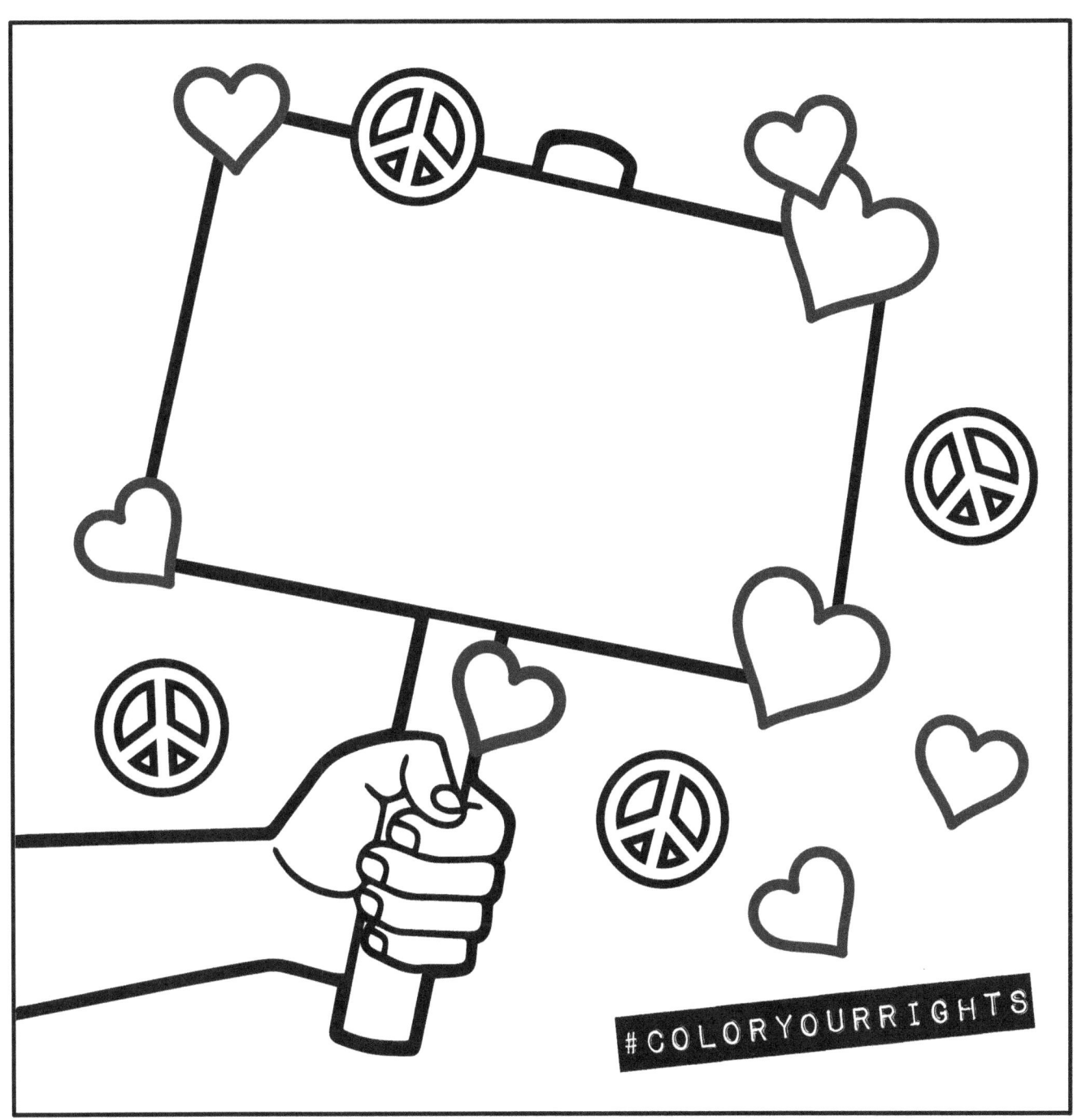

#COLORYOURRIGHTS

SHARE IT ON SOCIAL MEDIA
#COLORYOURRIGHTS
#COLORYOURRIGHTSCOLORINGBOOK
@COLORYOURRIGHTS

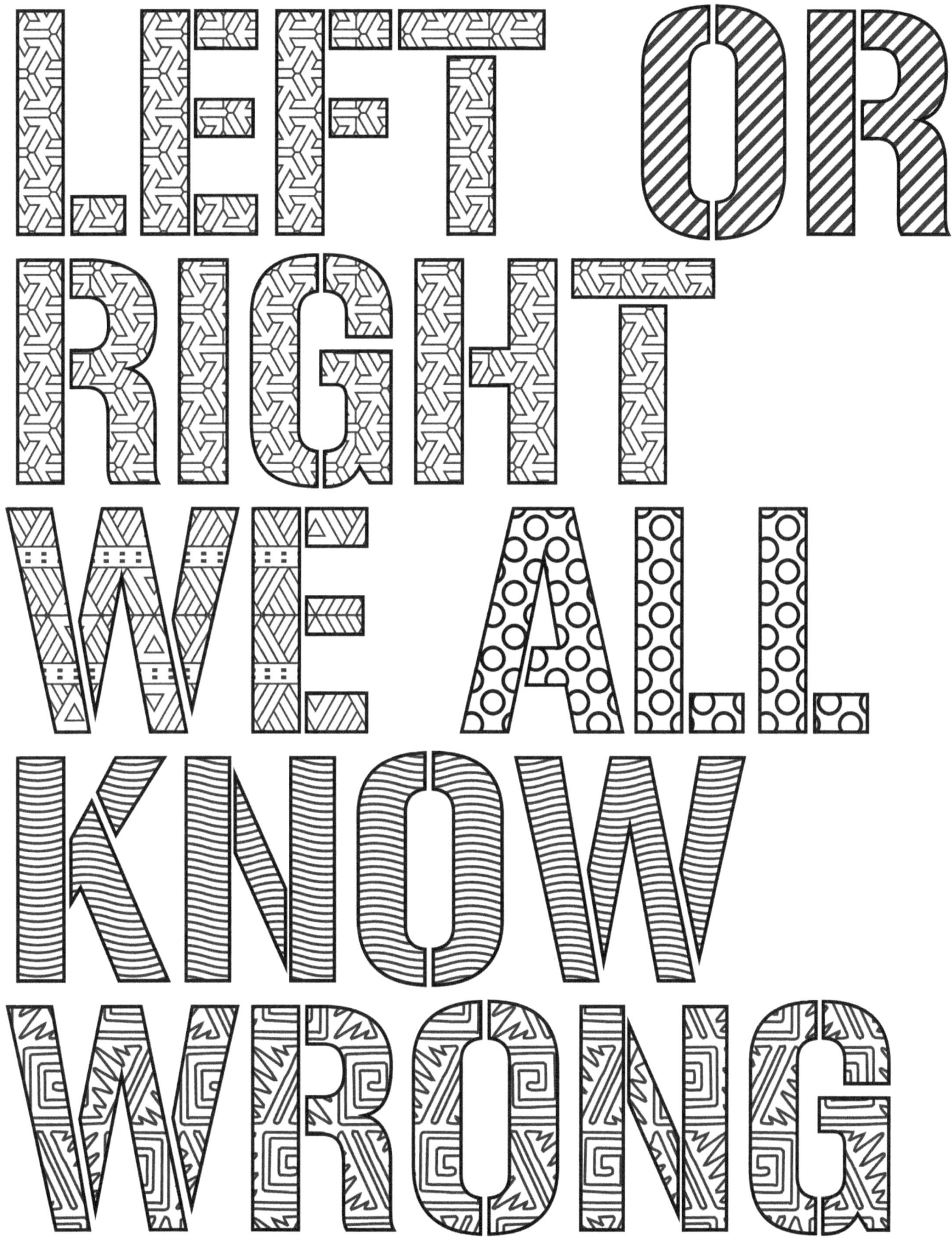

WE WILL NOT BE SILENCED

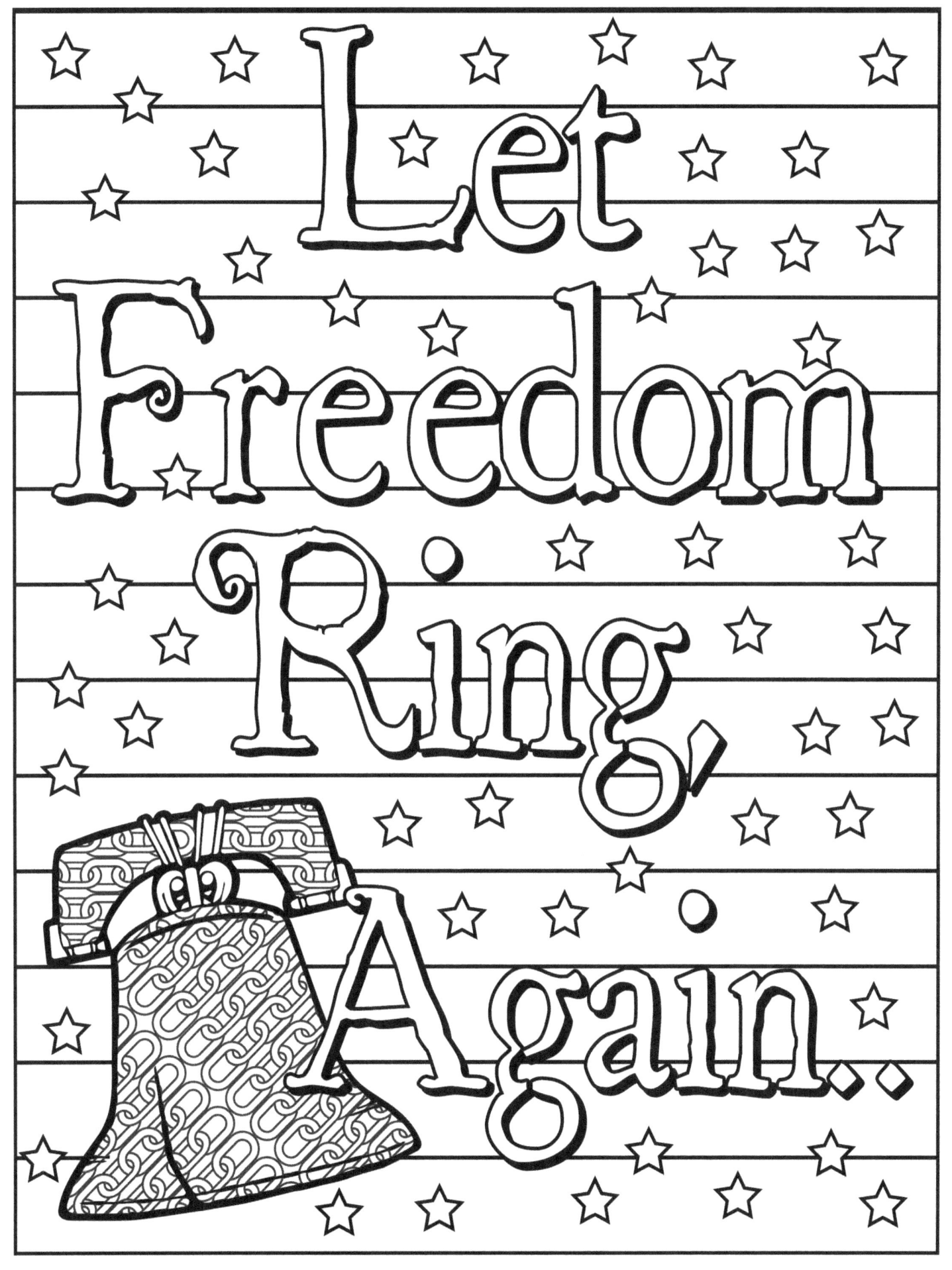

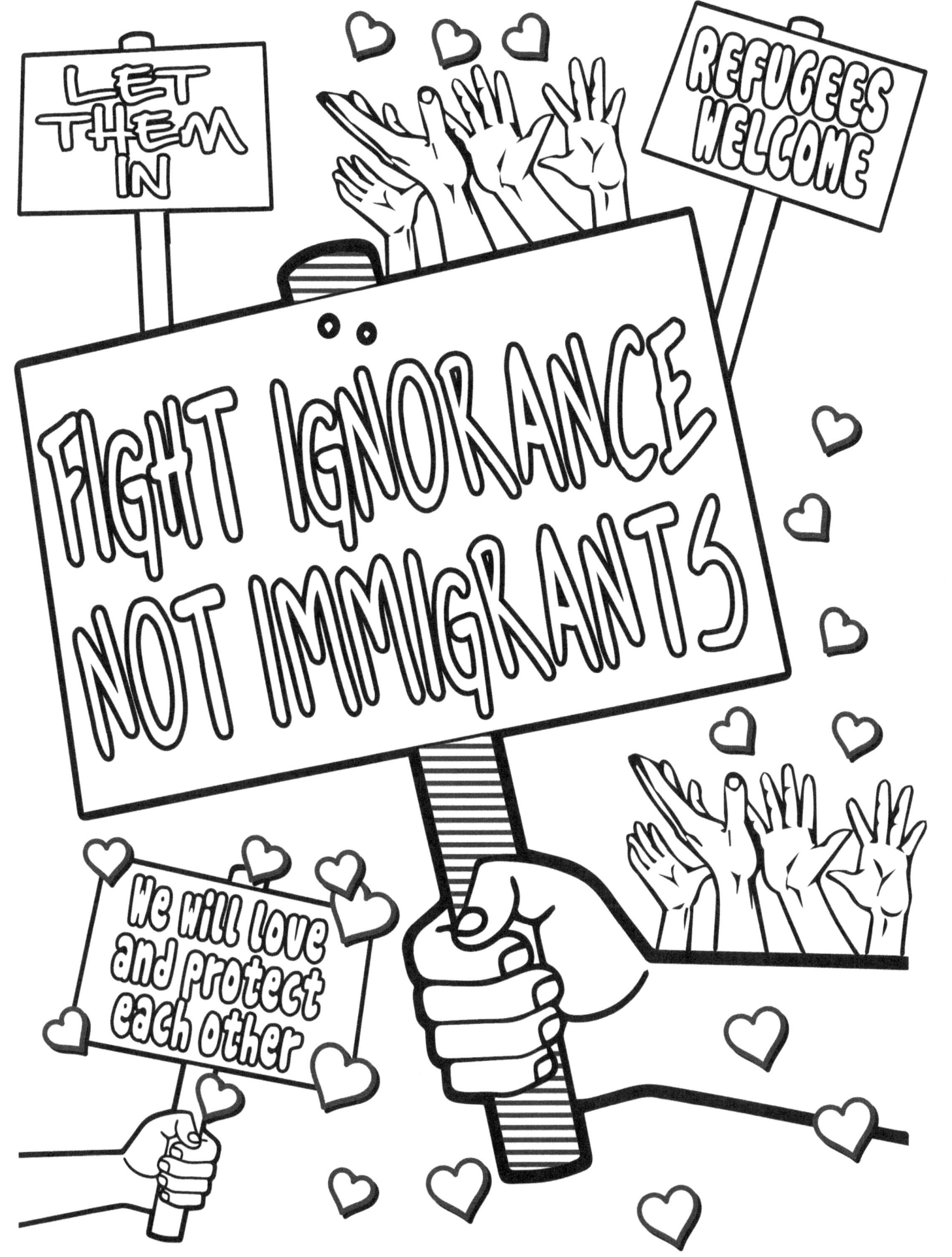

I WILL NOT apologize for who I AM

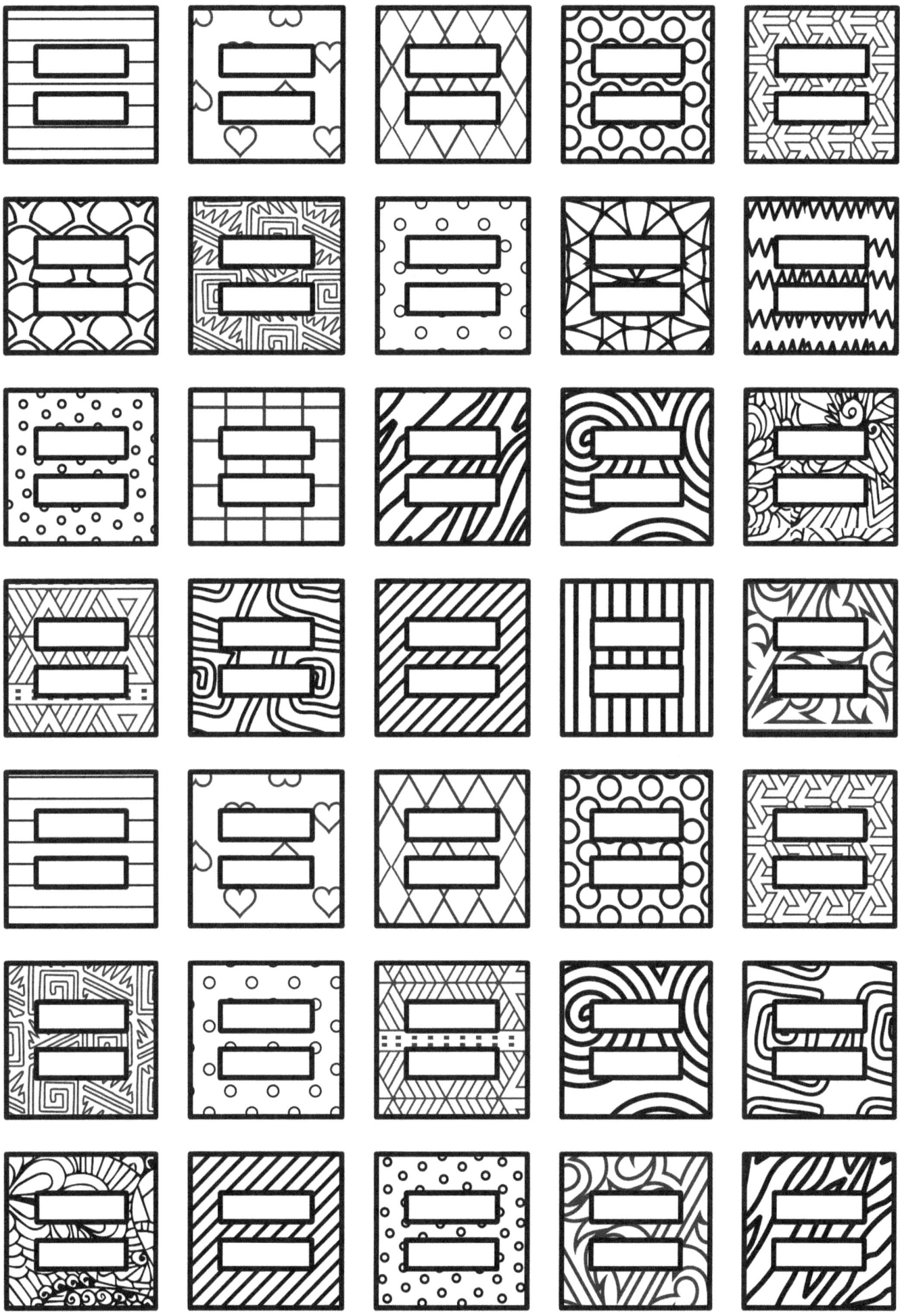

Express Yourself

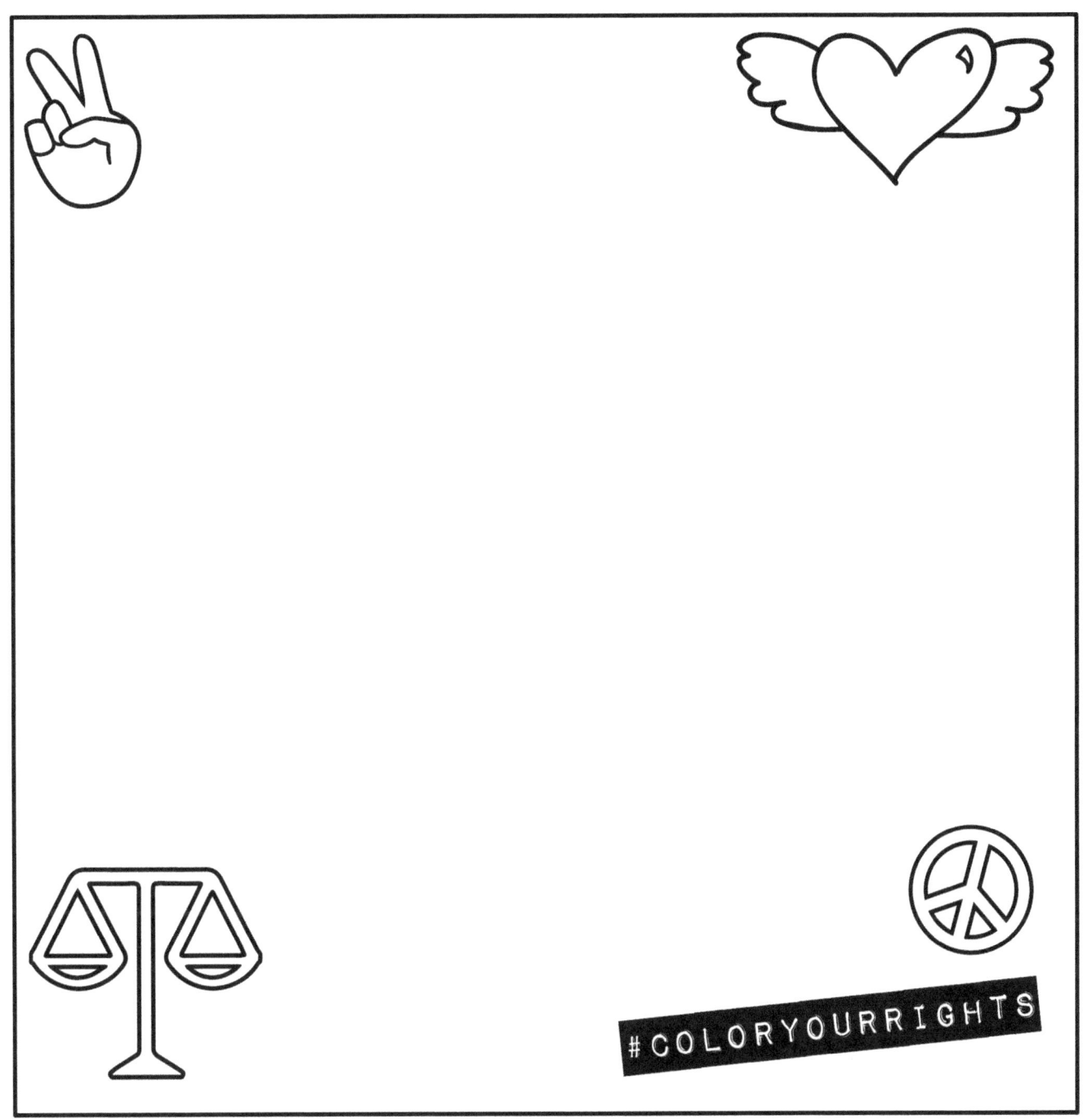

#COLORYOURRIGHTS

SHARE IT ON SOCIAL MEDIA
#COLORYOURRIGHTS
#COLORYOURRIGHTSCOLORINGBOOK
@COLORYOURRIGHTS

MAY I REMIND YOU THAT IT DOES NOT SAY R.S.V.P. ON THE STATUE OF LIBERTY

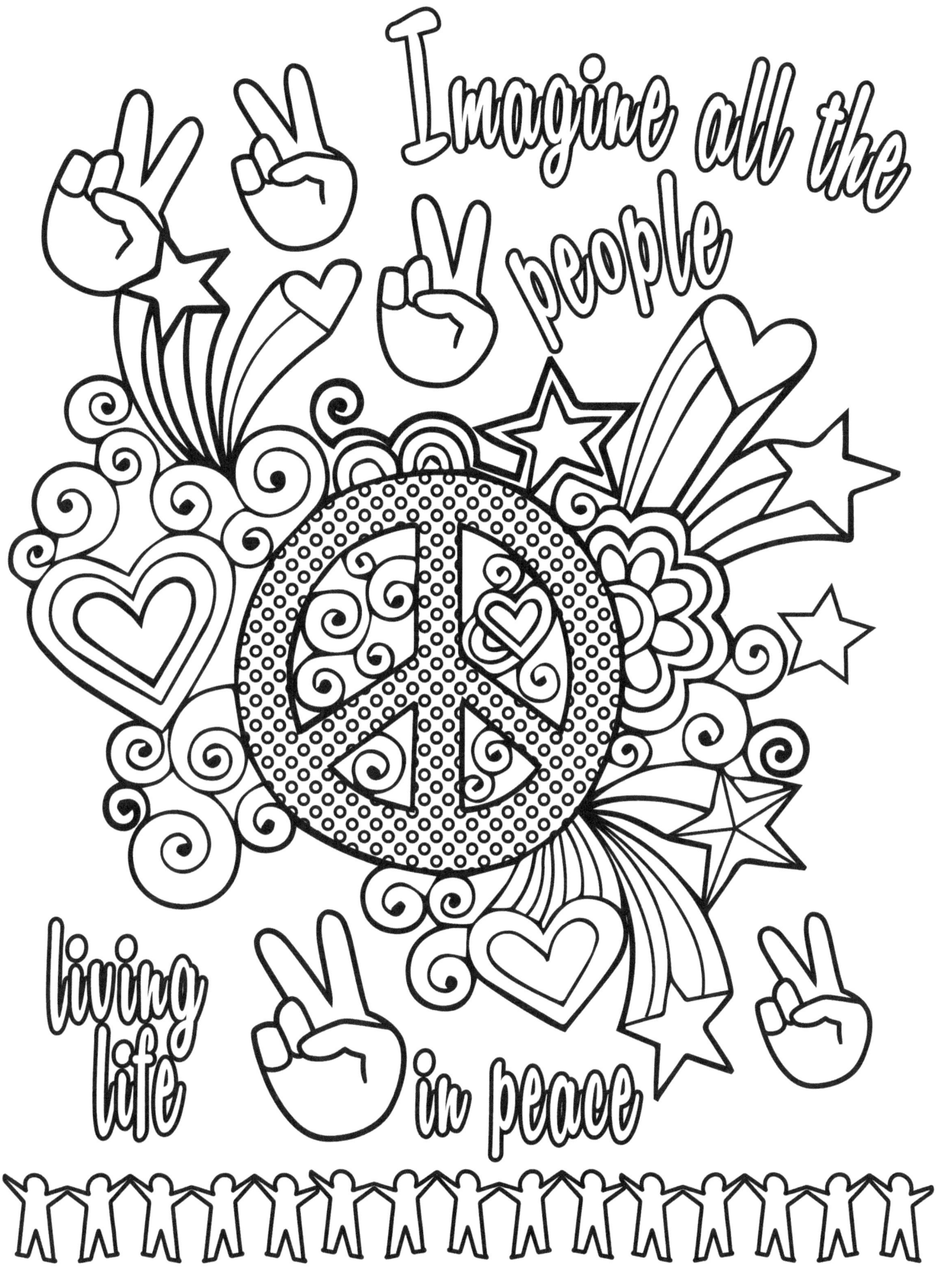

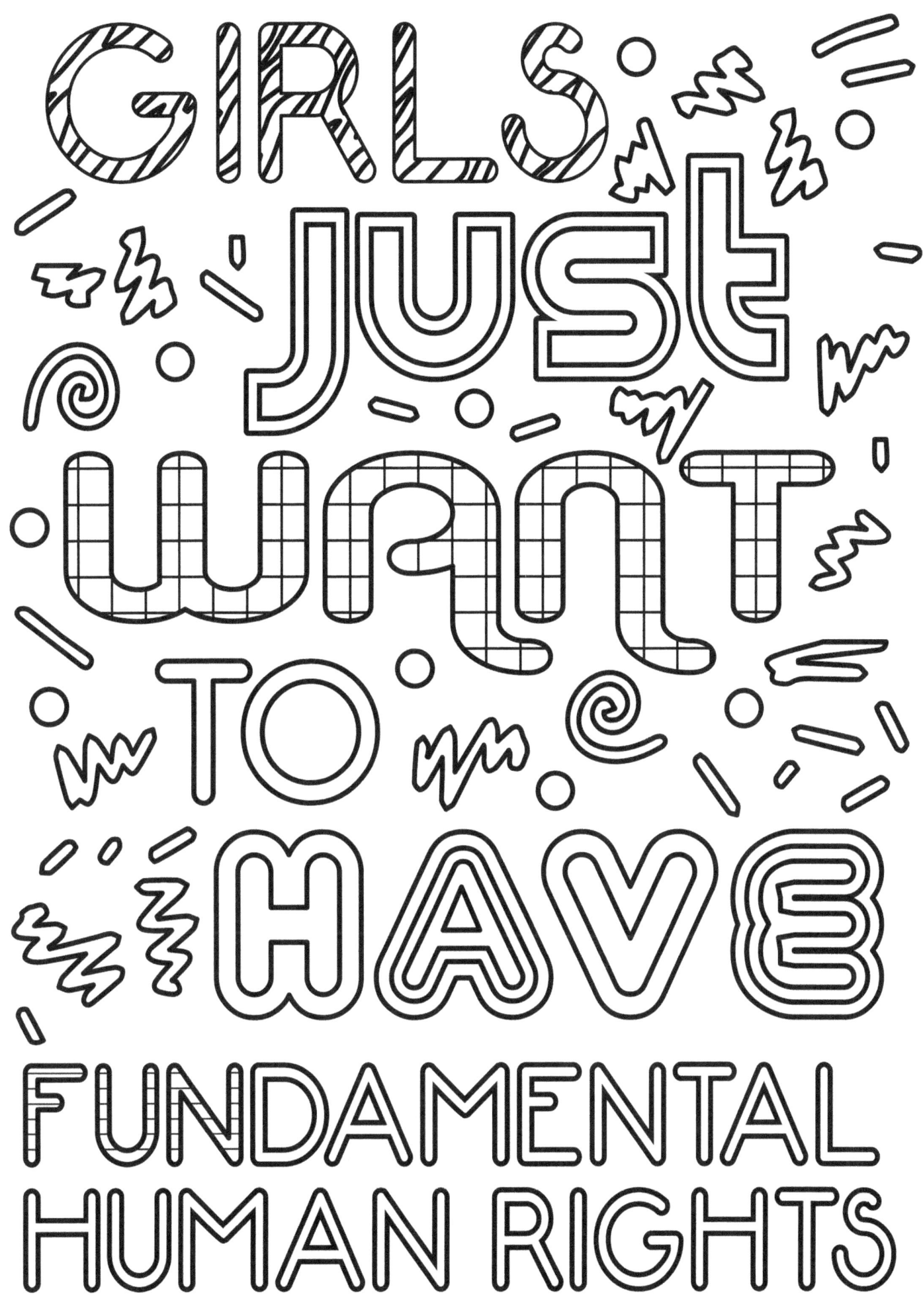

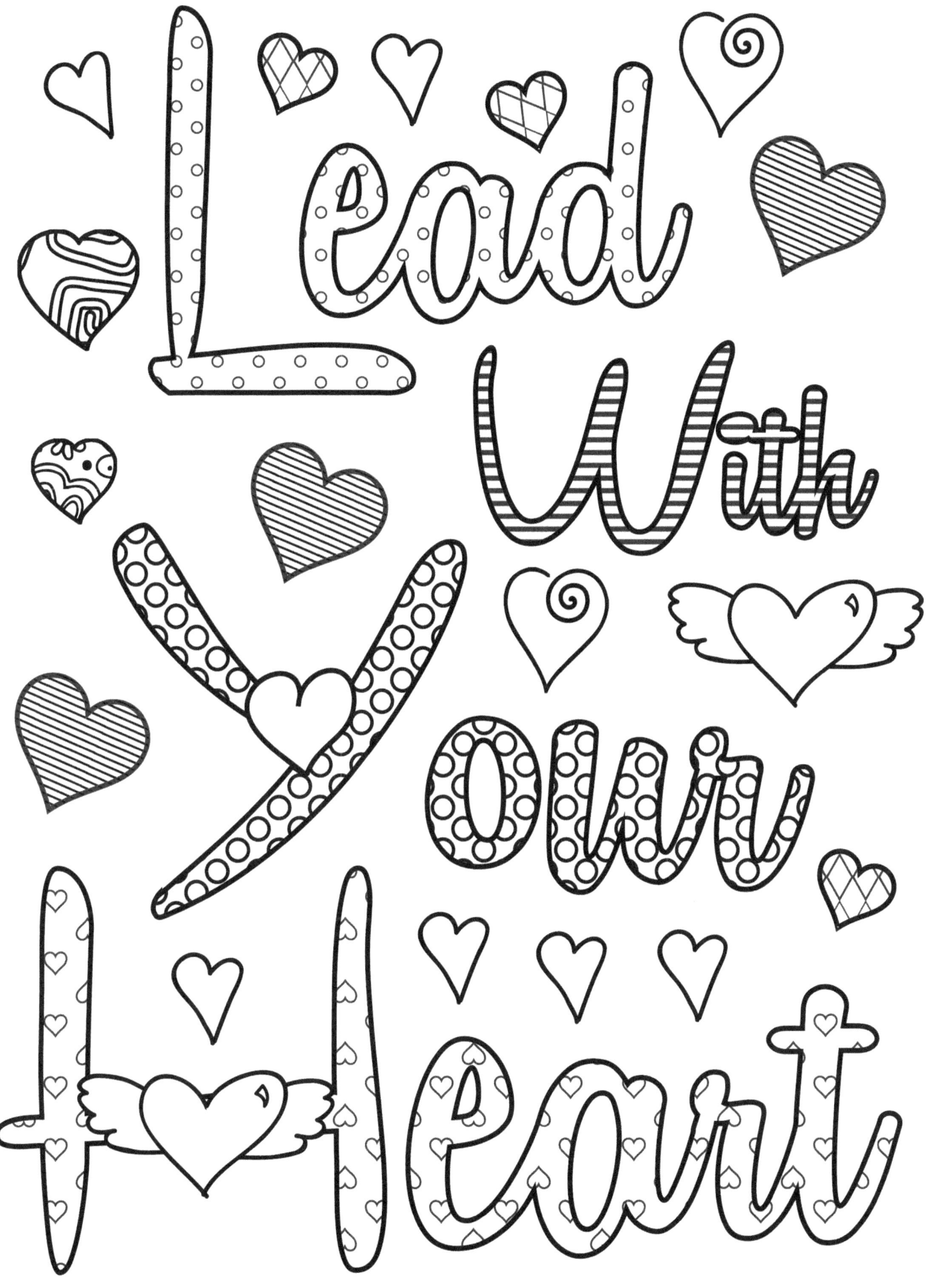

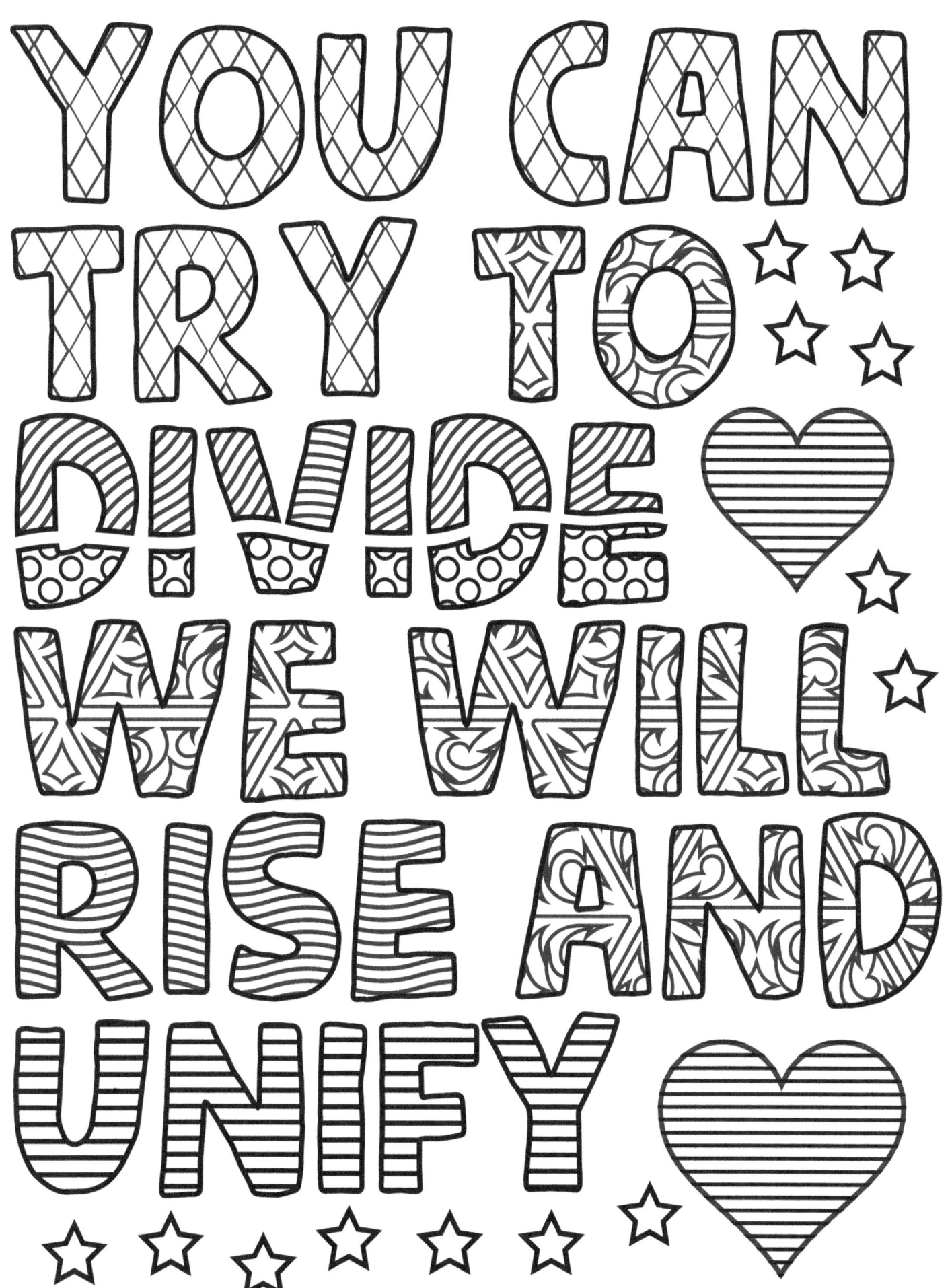

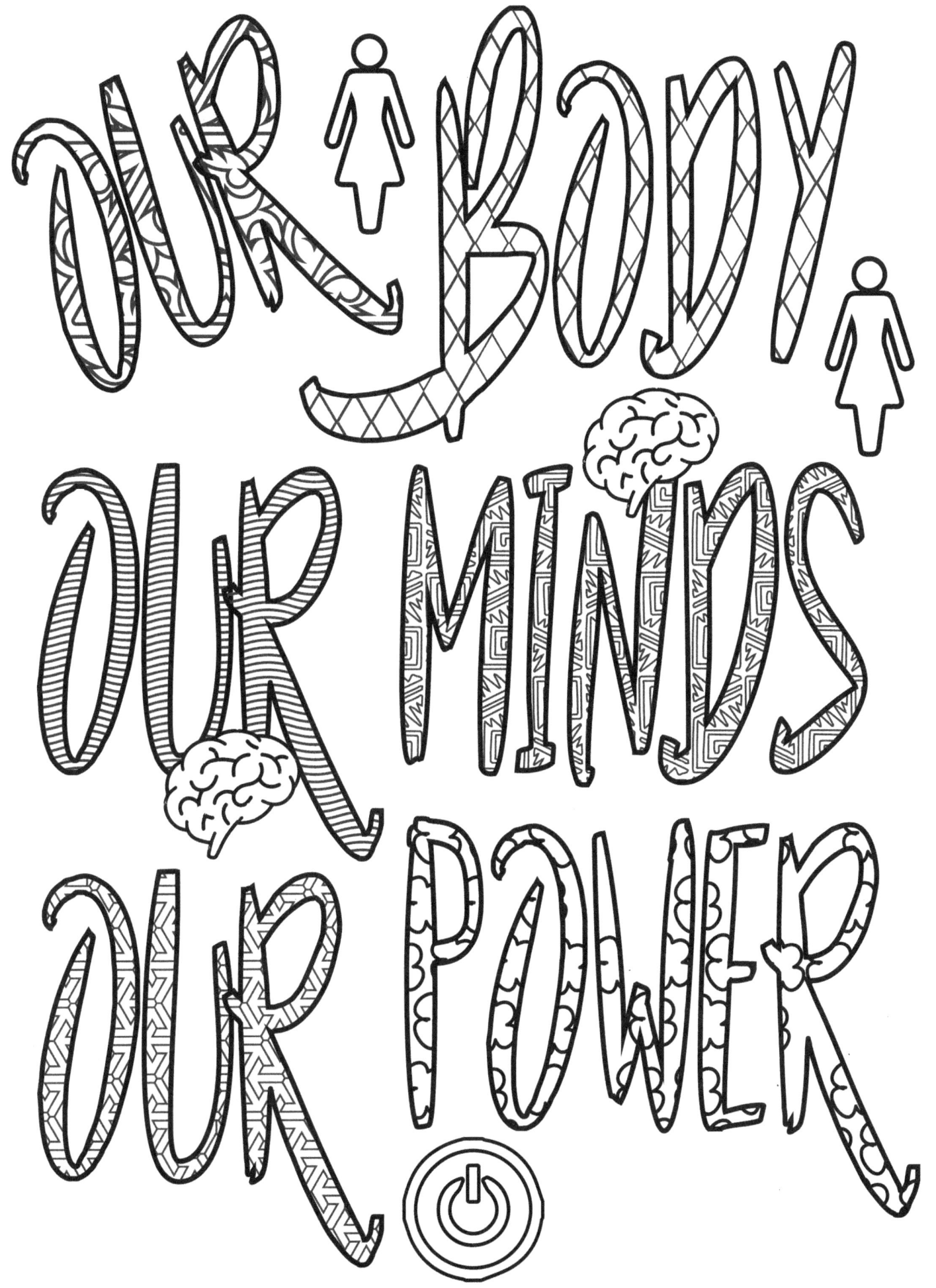

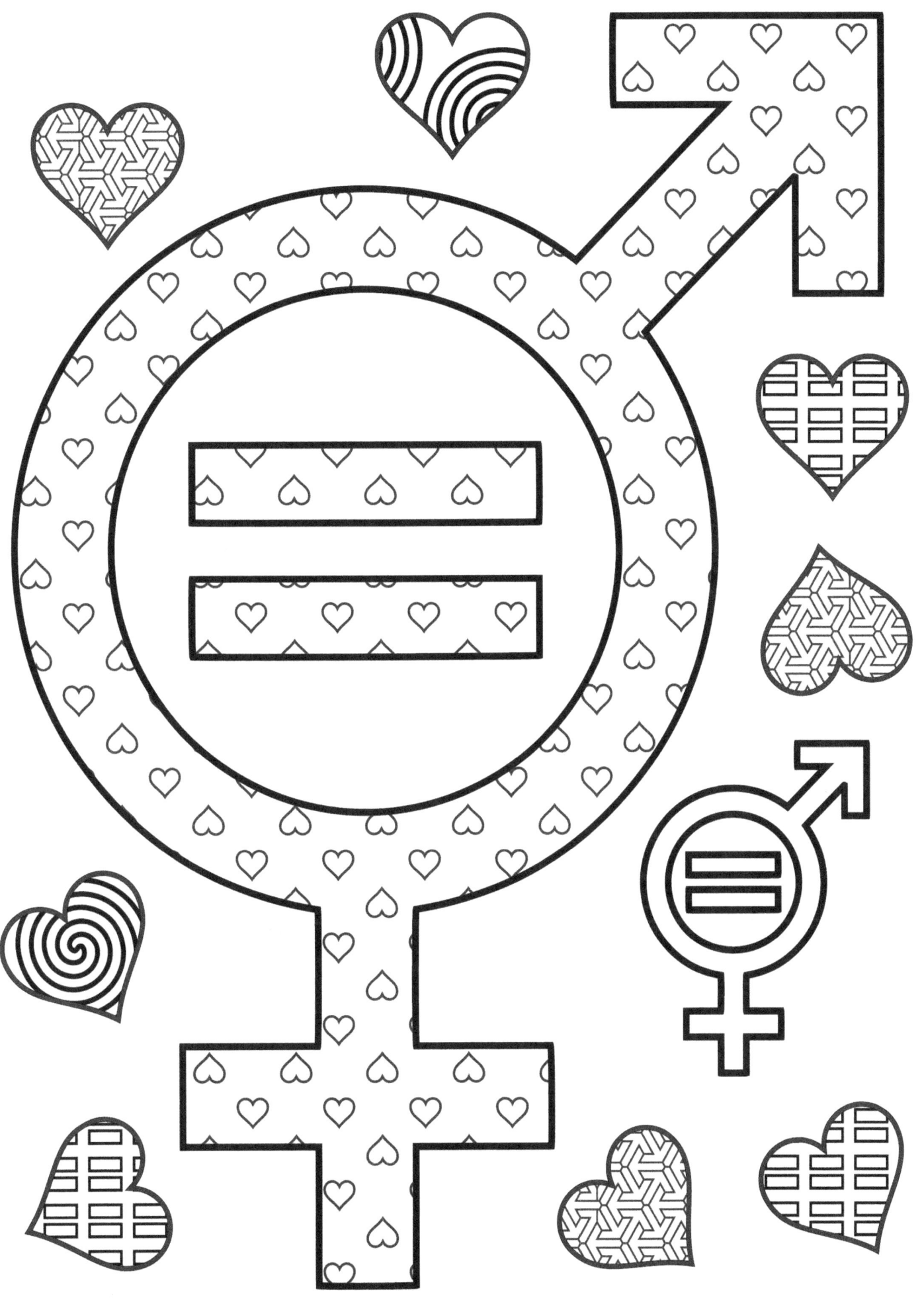

Express Yourself

SAY SOMETHING. DRAW IT. WRITE IT. OR TAKE A PICTURE AND TYPE IT.

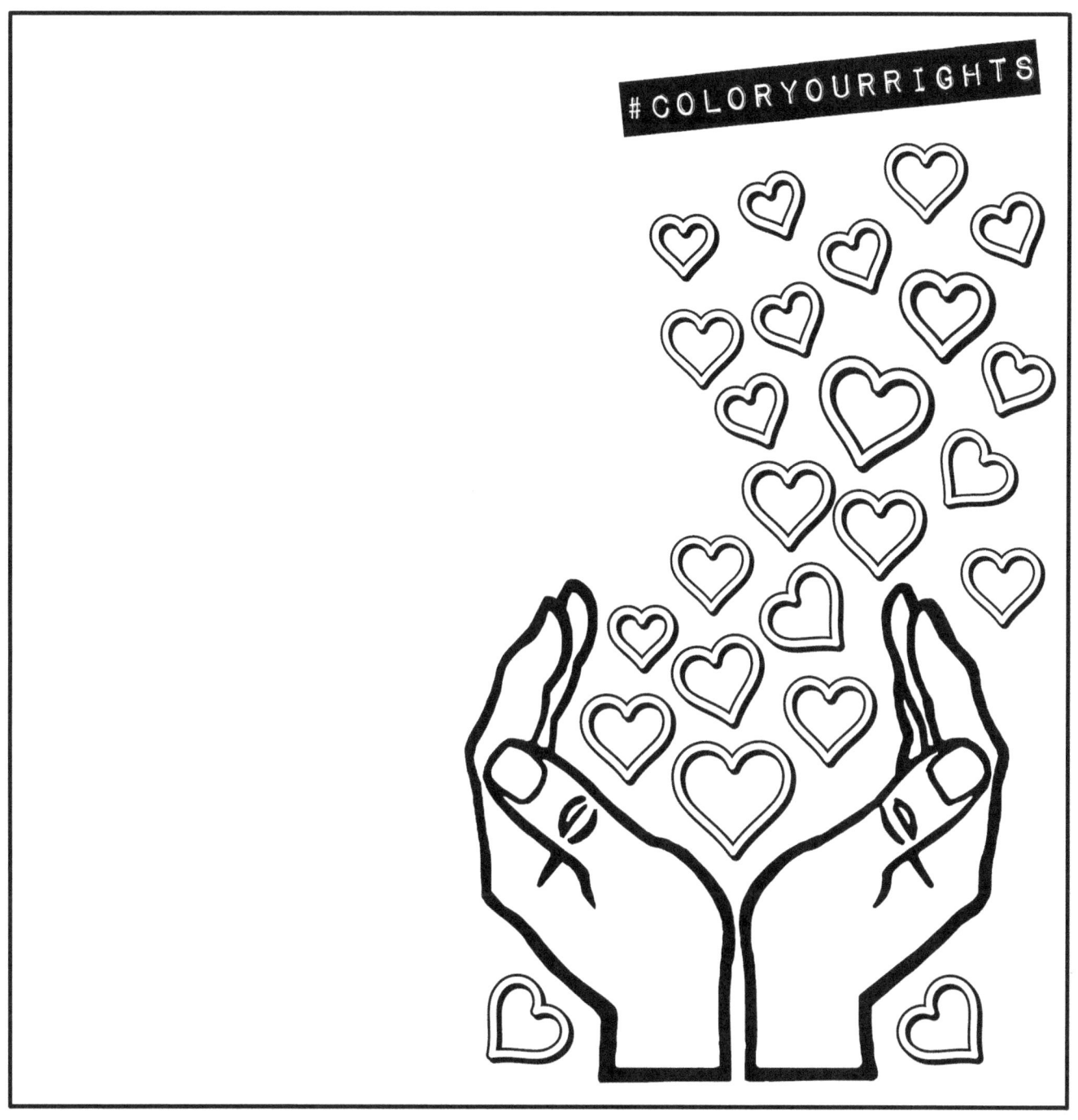

#COLORYOURRIGHTS

SHARE IT ON SOCIAL MEDIA

#COLORYOURRIGHTS

#COLORYOURRIGHTSCOLORINGBOOK

@COLORYOURRIGHTS

Express Yourself

SAY SOMETHING. DRAW IT. WRITE IT. OR TAKE A PICTURE AND TYPE IT.

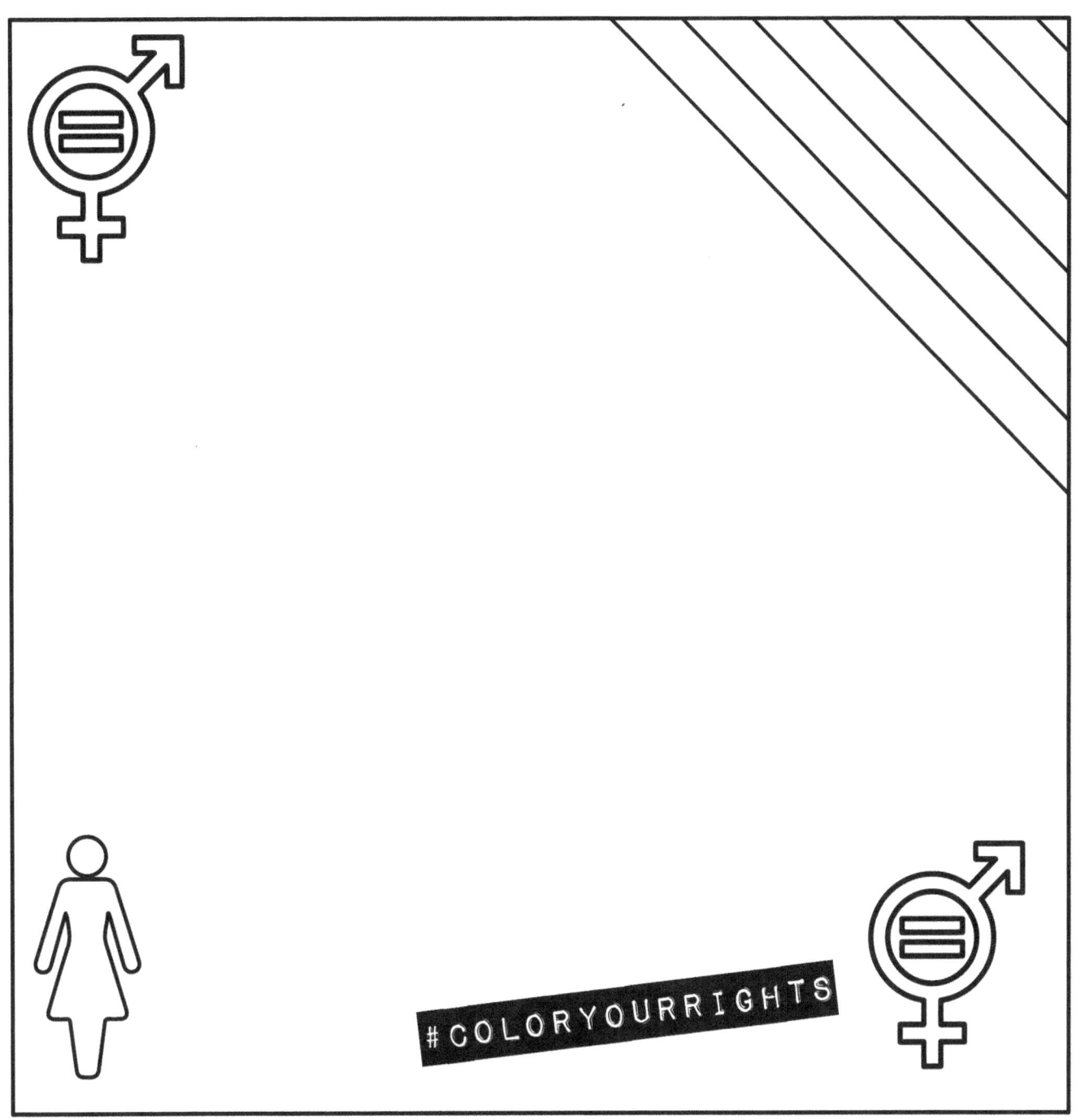

#COLORYOURRIGHTS

SHARE IT ON SOCIAL MEDIA
#COLORYOURRIGHTS
#COLORYOURRIGHTSCOLORINGBOOK
@COLORYOURRIGHTS

Express Yourself

I believe in

#COLORYOURRIGHTS

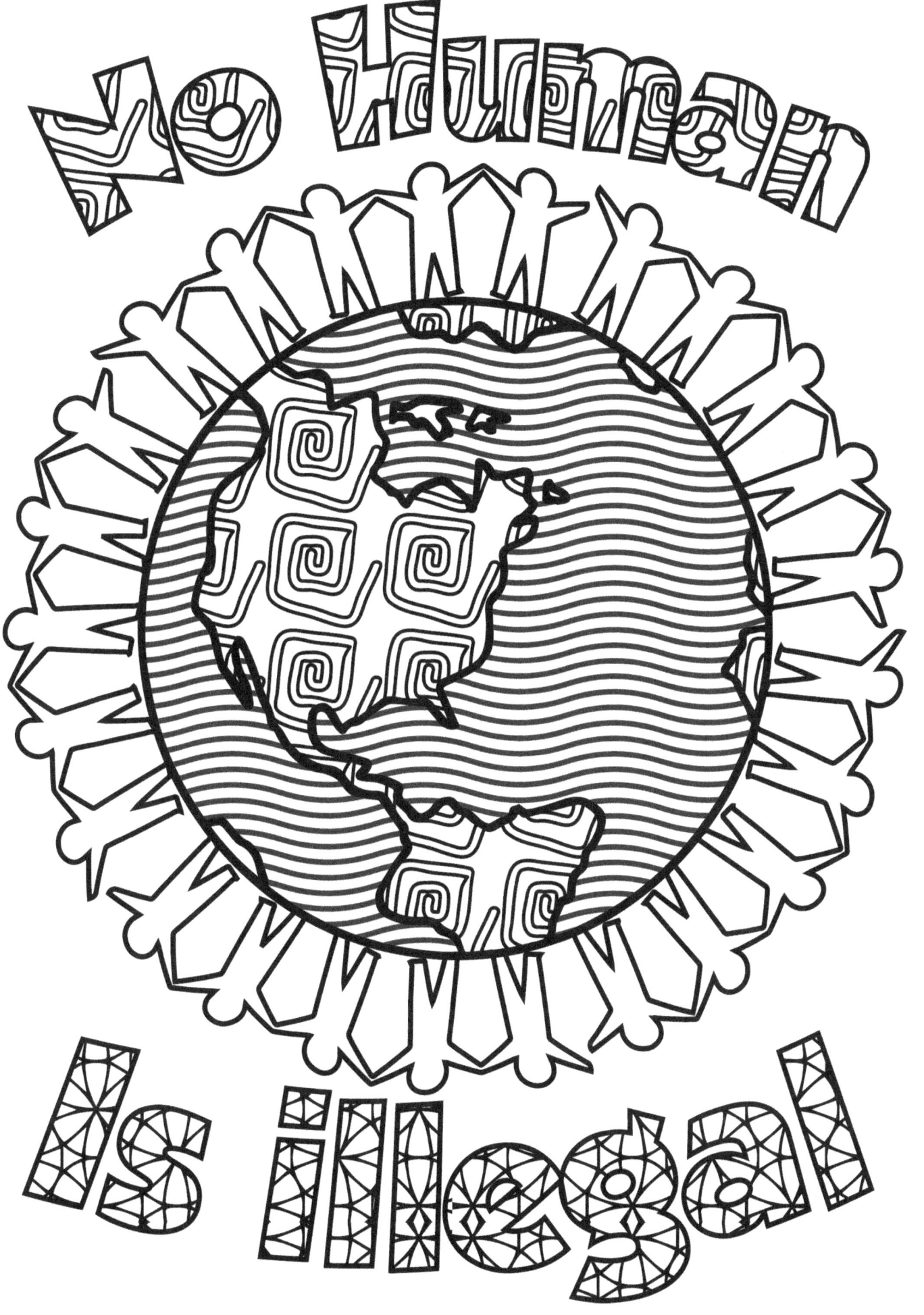

I AM ENOUGH. I'VE HAD ENOUGH! ENOUGH! ENOUGH IS ENOUGH !!

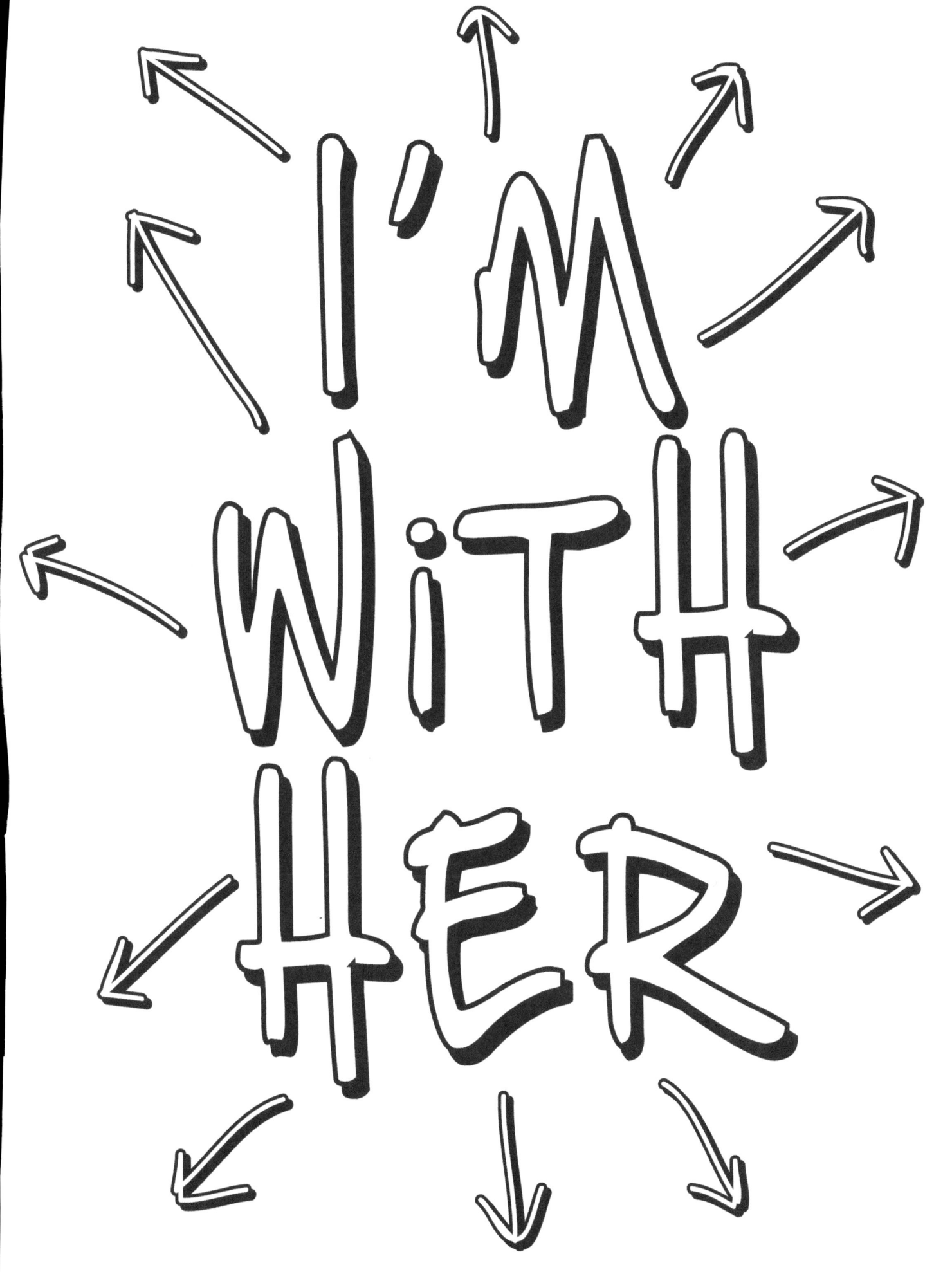